AF207203

HISTORY OF
SOCCER

KENNY ABDO

Fly!
An Imprint of Abdo Zoom
abdobooks.com

abdobooks.com

Published by Abdo Zoom, a division of ABDO, P.O. Box 398166, Minneapolis, Minnesota 55439. Copyright © 2020 by Abdo Consulting Group, Inc. International copyrights reserved in all countries. No part of this book may be reproduced in any form without written permission from the publisher. Fly!™ is a trademark and logo of Abdo Zoom.

Printed in the United States of America, North Mankato, Minnesota.
052019
092019

THIS BOOK CONTAINS
RECYCLED MATERIALS

Photo Credits: AP Images, Granger Collection, Icon Sportswire, iStock, Shutterstock, ©Hugo van Gelderen / Anefo p16 / CC0 1.0, ©Agência Brasil Fotografias p18 / CC BY 2.0
Production Contributors: Kenny Abdo, Jennie Forsberg, Grace Hansen
Design Contributors: Dorothy Toth, Neil Klinepier

Library of Congress Control Number: 2018963566

Publisher's Cataloging-in-Publication Data

Names: Abdo, Kenny, author.
Title: History of soccer / by Kenny Abdo.
Description: Minneapolis, Minnesota : Abdo Zoom, 2020 | Series: History of
    sports | Includes online resources and index.
Identifiers: ISBN 9781532127427 (lib. bdg.) | ISBN 9781532128400 (ebook) |
    ISBN 9781532128899 (Read-to-me ebook)
Subjects: LCSH: Soccer--History--Juvenile literature. | Football (Soccer)--Juvenile
    literature. | European football--Juvenile literature. | Sports--History--Juvenile
    literature.
Classification: DDC 796.33409--dc23

TABLE OF CONTENTS

SOCCER

Soccer has been played by everyone, from kids to pros, throughout the **centuries**. With more than 3 billion people watching the 2018 **World Cup**, soccer is the most beloved sport in the entire world.

Two teams of 11 players use their feet, head, and chest to get the ball down the field. Goalies can use their hands. The objective is to get the ball into the **opponent's** goal.

WARM UP

There have been many games like soccer throughout history. Historians think that the first form of soccer was played by the Chinese in the 2nd and 3rd **centuries**.

Balones de fútbol de las décadas de 1940 y 1950.
Footballs from the 1940s and 1950s.

10

Later, the game spread to countries like Japan, Greece, and Australia. Modern soccer was first played in 1863 in England. It was then that the Football Association was created. It was the first official **governing** body of soccer.

The International Federation of Association Football (FIFA) was formed in 1904. They organize the major soccer **tournaments** around the world.

INI INFANTINO

FIFA PRESIDENT

The biggest **tournament** is the FIFA **World Cup**. It is played every four years. The first one was held in Uruguay in 1930. The first Women's World Cup was played in China in 1991.

BIG SHOW

Brazilian soccer player Pelé is considered one of the greatest of all time. He was the youngest player to ever play in a **World Cup** at 17 years old. Pelé also **scored** an amazing 1,281 goals in his career!

Marta Vieira da Silva was voted the Best Women's player of 2018 by FIFA. She holds the Women's **World Cup** top-**score** record with 15 goals. Marta led the Brazilian national team to win the silver medal at both the 2004 and 2008 Summer **Olympics**.

Lionel Messi is thought to be the best player on the field today. He has fought his way to the **World Cup** an incredible 18 times. Through 2018, Messi had won the **European Golden Shoe** award a record five times!

GLOSSARY

century – an era of 100 years.

European Golden Shoe – an award given to the leading goalscorer of the season.

govern – to enforce the rules and laws.

Olympics – the biggest sporting event in the world that is divided into summer and winter games.

opponent – a rival team.

score – a collection of points to determine the winner and loser of a game.

tournament – a series of games played for a championship.

World Cup – an international soccer competition held every four years.

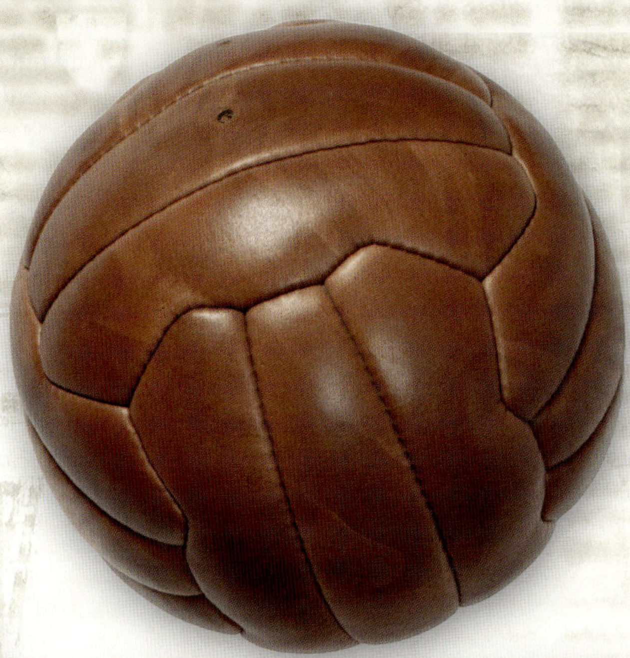

ONLINE RESOURCES

To learn more about soccer, please visit **abdobooklinks.com** or scan this QR code. These links are routinely monitored and updated to provide the most current information available.

INDEX